RIVER'S HEAVEN
A journey of self-discovery and introspection

Poetarrati

Volume 4

RIVER'S HEAVEN

A journey of self-discovery and introspection

Poetarrati

Volume 4

Ashok Subramanian

Highbrow Scribes Publications

New Delhi

Published 2024 by Highbrow Scribes Publications
Printed in New Delhi, India

ISBN: 978-81-956557-3-1

Highbrow Scribes Publications's mission is to foster a universal passion for reading by partnering with authors to help create stories and communicate ideas that inform, entertain, and inspire, and to connect them with readers everywhere.

Highbrow Scribes Publications books are printed on acid-free paper.

www.highbrowscribes.com

To Him, I surrender.

Om Namah Shivaya.

Dedicated to

My Mother

Contents

PART 3 : THE SEEKER: *Answers to the Seeking Soul*

PART 4 : Little Dose for the Heart

PART 5 : THREE MEN ON A BENCH: *The Weird And Wonderful World*

Preface

"The problem with introspection is that it has no end."

— *Philip K. Dick*

Nearly five decades of my life have not taught me about life than 2021. Last year surprised me with a serious COVID episode, and the deaths of my two loved ones.

What life taught me was the greatest lesson – to introspect. I used to introspect, but this year combined my introspection with my evolution as a poet and author. Introspection is the deep dive into the depths of one's inside – mind and soul. What we find there, is something we may not expect or even recognize.

"Many people suffer from the fear of finding oneself alone, and so they don't find themselves at all."

— *Rollo May, Man's Search for Himself*

The biggest fear that everybody has is not outside, but within. This journey within was mostly in solitude, with me staring at the space, often with tears, but also sometimes with crystal clear thoughts. This journey was not only in solitude and silence but also in suffering.

"But if these years have taught me anything it is this: you can never run away. Not ever. The only way out is in."

— *Junot Díaz, The Brief Wondrous Life of Oscar Wao*

In that suffering, silence, and solitude, it was clear to me that my journey to the inner recesses of my soul was to enlighten and emancipate myself. This journey was not to run away from me but to get me closer to myself.

"Have patience with everything that remains unsolved in your heart. ...live in the question."

— *Rainer Maria Rilke, Letters to a Young Poet*

The inward journey fueled by my curious introspection has made me realize that not everything can be answered immediately. But there is the time you go with the flow, like the river, living the question of life itself.

"A river unneeded still finds its way down to the ocean..."
— Will Advise

The noise in my head, mind, and soul may not be heard outside, but there were questions within and questions from what I had observed Unfortunately, the questions unanswered. But like the river, I flowed, till I reached a point where I saw my heaven at last. I knew that my journey would end, just like my mother's and father-in-law's did, where the netherworld is just a deep, salty abyss.

What is this? A River's Heaven.

From the ocean, starts another journey of the river's soul – as vapors into the clouds, and rains into the mountains. Then somewhere, at its origin, the river is born again.

Are our lives like the river? Will, we be back to flow again in another life? What about this life?

This book of poetry explores these questions and explodes with answers. I am sure that you have questions too.

~Ashok Subramanian

Acknowledgments

First I thank my **mother** for giving her best to make me what I am. Without you, Mom, I am nothing.

I thank my wife **Gayathri** and son **Anirudh** – In your own way, you have been the pillar of my life. And Anirudh, for bringing your special creativity, for doing all I asked, as ever.

To **Priya Patel**, who has appreciated my poems and poetry reviews, and who has taken the time to review and share her valuable inputs.

To **Highbrow Scribes Publications** and **Amazon** doing an amazing job of delivering high-quality E-books and paperbacks in India, the US, and the globe.

PART 1
RIVER'S HEAVEN
Discovering Self in Nature

River's Heaven

Image by Antonios Ntoumas from Pixabay

Born in the high mountain
I end up in the mighty ocean.
Should I be happy and full of bliss
When my heaven is the salty
abyss.

A journey forward and beyond
As vapor into the clouds
As rains into the mountains
Somewhere, I am born again.

Fickle Of The Mighty

Why are oceans deep
Yet occasionally turbulent
And waves washup ashore?

Why is the sky vast
Yet flashes lightning
And throws up thunder?

Why are mountains tall
Yet spew molten lava
Consuming lives around?

Why is the sun a life giver
Yet flares up to kill
With drought and fires?
Why are our minds large
Yet utter those words
That we regret?

Perhaps nature is that
The mighty can be fickle
Once in a while.

Survival Of The Butterfly

Beautiful it may be
But a butterfly seeking nectar
From a beautiful flower
Is still an act of survival.

Conceit

The thorn thinks
It's protecting the rose

But it has no idea that
It's just a prick.

Early Morning Thoughts

Early morning thoughts about you
Pure and pristine yet fleetingly disappear
Like how the sun consumes the dew.

Image by kie-ker from Pixabay

Magic Of The Sky

Treachery

Image by Mystic Art Design from Pixabay

One of the collective nouns for a group of ravens is 'treachery'.
An inspired Haiku.

The absence of the nightingale's
Melodious music replaced by boisterous cacophony
In the treachery of ravens.

Tree Speak

Pic by Janrye at Pixabay

My hairfollicles stood up against a quiet chill;
The cold wind stopped that it won't freeze;
The trees and leaves now stood still
In the absence of the usual breeze.

As the sky lit up slowly with a reluctant yellow;
The winter sun, at the east, now sober and mellow;
I took the first steps for my morning walk
Listening to music or some wise talk.

I looked up the trees that I passed under
Why were they quiet and silent? I wonder.
Were they meditating like the great sages—
For they were standing through the ages?

A gentle breeze set in out of the blue,
Shaking the trees, as they waved at me,
The tree showered, on me, its yellow flowers a few,
I looked up and smiled with rampant glee.

Another walk below the tree, that dawn,
A crow woke up, crowing its yawn,
Stretching and answering its nature's call
Just missing me, I saw its poop fall.

Was the same tree that sprayed the flowers
Now blessing me with the crow's poop showers
Sharing the wisdom of the past great masters
That our lives are filled with triumphs and disasters.

Little did I know that the tree would answer
And it took sometime for me to discover
The answers for questions I would never seek
All I had to do was listen to the tree speak.

Bridge To Heaven

Pic by Adalhelma at Pixabay

She smiled at the orchids, roses and daffodils.
They smiled at her like a thousand mirrors.
Her image in thousand blossoms,
All fresh faced and smiling.

Ah! the butterflies and birds
Hopping on the flowers and trees
Mirrored her joyous heart beat
A quiet party was beginning then.

The breeze asked her – can I join?
As she nodded her exquisite head
The flowers followed nodding in tandem
The breeze caressed them all softly.

The sun followed – was it too late?
It is still day, Sir – she said.
The rays exuded the warmth and shine
Just enough to brighten the day.

Ah! there was that passing cloud
Stunned by this gorgeous scene.
"I may as well join"– it said, and got the nod,
The drizzle started, shining and swaying.

Who would miss such a party,
When bow of colors seven
Appeared at the edge of the sky
Like a bridge to heaven.

Innocence

Image by Oberholster Venita from Pixabay

Innocence is Utopian only if
a gardener fences the garden
and fosters the flowers
but he lets them be.

Flowers are still pure
after the bees touch them
yet they are spoiled
when the gardener smells.

The Rose And The Weed

The yellow rose preened and swayed in the warm June air,
'I am the pet and the diva of the balcony garden',
It proudly announced, to nobody in particular,
As no other flower blossomed in the warm summer.

One fine morning, a little sapling appeared besides,
The rose did not notice, as it seldom,
'dour green first, then one morning much taller,
Another morning, it stood taller than the rose itself.

The rose is still a rose, and it scoffed with hatred to the bone,
'Await your guillotine, you ugly Goliath', in a derisive tone.
'The Gardener will cut you down to size,'
She warned 'Don't expect him to be nice.'
The green plant kept his sanity and stead

Not a shout, a silence response instead
Quietly growing taller by the day,
It was noticed by the Gardener one day.

'Ah! This weed!' exclaimed the lord and master,
'A beast near the beauty, and growing ever faster,
I shall remove you in just a moment.'
To fetch the sickle and shovel, he went.

The resolute Gardener sighed and heaved,
His torso toiled, and his mind peeved.
Quiet a struggle, the green giant put,
Deep in the soil, intertwined its roots.

'Finally,' said the Gardener, the green plant in his hands,
'I told you,' the rose twisted and twirled into a dance,
'I am the queen here,' and 'you are a weed.'
'Wrong time, you ugly, wrong place to grow, indeed.'

A young boy passing by running an errand,
Tiny palms took the weed from his calloused hand,
The Gardener bid him to throw it away,
The young man interjected, 'Sir, if I may.'

A little bit of rain and a singing lark,
A rainbow somewhere in the western sky,
When the boy took the plant to the corner dark,
He planted the weed, where eyes do not pry.

The Gardener watched the boy awhile,
And questioned him with a wicked smile.
'What is the point in saving the weed,
A plant that is wicked and there is no need?'

'Sir,' said the young boy wise,' Maybe you can explain!'
'My questions that are simple and plain.'
As he looked at the rose shining and clean
And weed at the distance, that the Gardener had weaned.

'Sir, for this garden, aren't you the watch and warden,
Why is a rose different from others then?'
'Are not all flora and foliage equal in the God's Garden,
That we behold in our eyes wide and minds open?'

'Sir, pardon me, for such a silly question from this child.'
Would the weed not be equal to the rose, in the wild?'
The weed too has life, in the wisdom I garnered,
So I planted it away from the rose, in the garden corner.'

'My child, your words are worldly wise, and mature,
And your thoughts are indeed pristine and pure.'
The discrimination reflects this poor human's mind,
Such a thought you will not find in any other kind.'

'To choose one above the other,
Is never the nature of any mother.'
'Will a human gardener ever understand,
That garden is just a piece of land?'

The Gardener looked away with tears in his eyes,
Learning the lesson from nature and the child wise,
How could he explain this to his owner? - his mind froze,
That in his garden, shall exist, both the weed and the rose.

PART 2
BROKEN MIRROR:
The Fragmented Self

Broken Mirror

Image by creatifrankenstein from Pixabay

Mirror showing my angry face
Crashed and broke on the bathroom floor
Showing hundreds of angry ME.

Silent Eyes

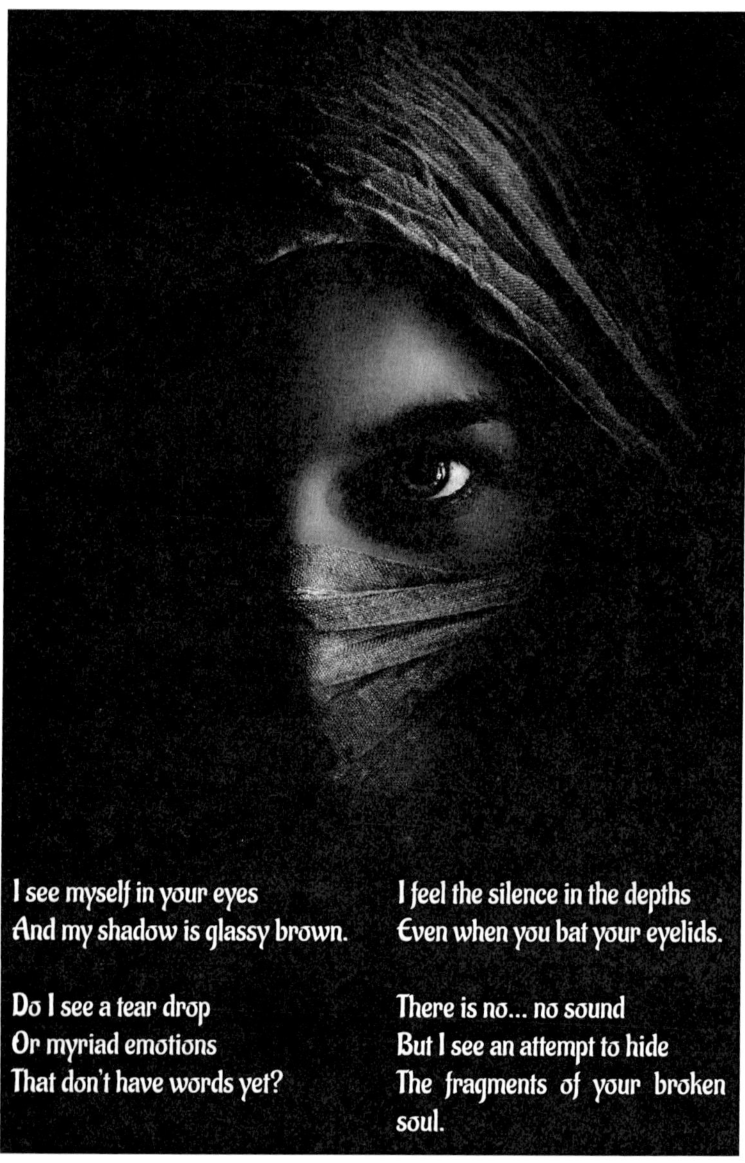

I see myself in your eyes
And my shadow is glassy brown.

Do I see a tear drop
Or myriad emotions
That don't have words yet?

I feel the silence in the depths
Even when you bat your eyelids.

There is no... no sound
But I see an attempt to hide
The fragments of your broken
soul.

A Road To Nowhere

Like a river just born
In the lap of the mountains
Yet to discover its ocean!

But the ocean knows
It will return the rains
To the mountains!

Like the rains that form
In the womb of the clouds
Yet to discover where they drop!
But the monsoon winds
That carry the rains know
Where they seek their own landfall!

My journey of life
Began inside my mother
Yet to discover my end!

But who will tell me
Where I am heading, as I travel on
A road to nowhere?

Totem

Sleep well and drift
But we shall find your totem
In a world of chaos.

Mental Tempest

Image by Myriams-Fotos from Pixabay

A boat without a sail
Tossed around by stormy waves.
On a day of mental tempest.

Moon

Image by Viola ' from Pixabay

Even if you wane
Hiding behind your own shadow
You are still the moon.

Scars And Stars

I did it because of you – he said
What to do, it repeats every day
Don't want to turn up, yet
I will do it because you wanted me to.

Cat whistles and hoots
I became the toast of their lunch breaks
I try to mock at myself
but it gets me more

I find that store room to be alone
And text the one person I can
But you are the one who put me in
So, I implore you, at least just listen, please.

Few more days, everybody says
Get over the pain and get the certificate
And the pain will be long gone
And the achievement will stay

But did anybody notice that
While chasing the stars
I cry inside yet smile
So that nobody can notice my scars.

Empty Garden

All too sudden
Flowers blown away
By gusts of wind;

Or plucked vigorously
By an invisible hand
Of a devious mind;

Was a bloom yesterday,
A devastation today
A story most unkind;

What would remain?
Whose turn is next?
Answers we cannot find.

Shock of today
Anxiety about tomorrow
Leading a life blind.

A life so fickle
The empty garden
Quietly does remind.

Lost And Found

The mind searches for the last image of where we left them,
The visuals and the walkthroughs that we attempt to cobble together
About the beloved thing or the thing that we needed
But somewhere lost when we seek or need it.
When we remember we go to the place we forgot
And search there - it is the same place, but it is long past.
If we get it, the delight of finding the lost object
Else the desperate search, visualizing and trying to remember
At some point, we will all give up on it that could never be found.
Life goes on, some with fond memories and others with regret
Yet in the long run, we could live without it for better or for worse.

It is the same about a person when they leave us
For short periods or for longer, forever or for good
When we try to cling to them we still can't
For life goes on, or else death takes them away
If they are alive there is a possibility to reunite or meet
But it is the same body but a different person;

This time changed and weathered by Father Time;
Yet we expect them to be like they were
Like how we had them in our memories;
The person has gone or changed if we meet again.

Our fickle minds play tricks, bringing pain, joy and sorrow
Just because we bury our head in the sands of time;
To understand that people change for better or for worse
So will we ever find what we thought we had lost?

PART 3
THE SEEKER
Answers to the Seeking Soul

The Seeker

Image by Tumisu from Pixabay

I walked alone
In a crowd of people
And found myself.

Rise And Fall

Image by: Rise and Fall Image by Jonathan Reichel from Pixabay

Some words of Chinese wisdom
When your ascension starts
Does your descension too –
For beyond the peak
Is the deep dark valley
and folks, that is 'rise and fall'.

In my limited wisdom I would say
When your descension starts
There is an ascension too –
For beyond the deep dark valley
Is a tall peak to climb
and folks, that is 'fall and rise'.

The Younger Me

Image by Stefan Keller from Pixabay

I put my trembling hand
On my wrinkled forehead
To pull out the younger me,
From my childhood memory.
To ask just one question
If you were to meet me
And see what I am –
Will you be happy?

The child thought and thought
And answered thus, 'Only for this
I fought.'
'I have no doubt, not a shroud,
This journey I am proud.'

'You are, where you should be
To become you from me;
There is nothing to dread
About the path between us, I
tread.'

'A journey that has seen many
wars
And full of wrinkles and scars;
Those signatures of time
All part of a story sublime.'

I put my hand on my forehead
And the creases disappeared
A world now better understood
And I, a lot wiser, for good.

The Hell In Your Mind

Image by Gerd Altmann from Pixabay : The Hell in Your Mind

You don't need to visit hell. You can create it in your own mind. Or not.

Hell is in your mind
It is in this life, not after;
It is your own making
Or it just happens to you.

It burns within like a cauldron.
The sky is no more azure;
The thoughts are like grey clouds
Pregnant with problems.

Colliding inside vociferously;
Creating myriad thunderous conflicts

And sparks of anger emanate
Like the furious bolts of lightning.
And when the fury spills over

Through your red eyes
Now raining unabashed
Only this time, in salty tears.

Again, to flood the mental landscape
And common sense drowns
And sinks to the bottom
In the unfathomable deluge.

With a little breeze in your lungs
I mean, a deep breath,
The stormy clouds are blown away
No more rain, thunder, or lightning.

Somewhere the flashflood recedes
Revealing the sunk sense again
This time, with sediments of sanity
Shining in your tear—washed face.

Music Of Life

Image by Viki_B at Pixabay.

Just listen for a moment
The sounds of your heartbeat and breath
Are Music of your Being.

The Sailor And The Wind

Image by Michael Schwarzenberger from Pixabay

The gentle breeze is fine;

But finding which way the wind blows

Helps me set my sail.

Originality

Image by M. H. from Pixabay

Don't strive to be unique

Because you are the only original

No copy is ever better.

Life In Colors

Picture by TheDigitalArtist at Pixabay

Born out of the blue:
Life is anything but black and white
Finally our hair turns grey.

Questions To My Teacher

My dear teacher,
A few questions to ask
On my journey as student
Beyond my routine tasks.

Do I learn
That all you can teach me ?
Or do you also learn
while you teach me?

Are you feeling
Filled to the brim
Or like the leaves of the garden
that wait to be trimmed?

Do you see a higher branch
That you can reach,
Unlearn and learn new things
Every time you teach?

Will you fill me, dear teacher,
Of the things, to you known?
Do you seek answers
Or you impart your own?

Is my learning from you
About only discovering the new
But also to think deep,
Discern and chew?

Do I learn from you
Oh! The teacher I respect,
Or do I learn with you
And together we introspect?
Oh my teacher! Dear,

Help me keep my mind steady,
For I am told –
A teacher shall appear
when the student is ready.

Breathe

Breath in!
A bit of universe travels inside us.
A morsel of air,
Fueling our bodies
And nourishing our souls.

Breath out.
A bit of us travels out to the universe.

An acceptance of our carbon filled excretion.

A two directional highway.
The highway of life.
Designed to be involuntary and forgotten.

Taking away a responsibility from us
Yet propelling us forward in our lives.
A silent miracle of nature,
For the journey of our lifetime.

Valentine

While searching for my valentine,
I stopped and looked at my mirror
And found my missing soul mate.

Today

Image by JohnArtsz from Pixabay

There is no day more beautiful than today,
For we can still do the things we dream about,
Or still dream about the things that we want to do,
Or simply watch the beautiful blue marble
Roll around the large fiery one.

Divine

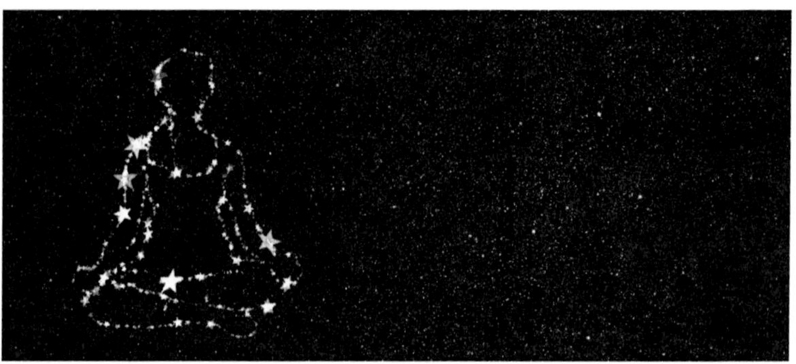

Pic by geralt from Pixabay

You are your eternal divine
Blissful and loving, courageous and calm
Search for your answers within.

My Mentor

I searched for my mentor
But never found him!
Time passed by
And still... never found him!
A day came when I paused
And looked back ...
It was me, stupid,
That I was searching for...

Words And Currencies

Image by kalhh from Pixabay

If words were currencies
My mind, the minting factory
My silence, the savings bank,
My books, treasure troves,
And I, Robinson Crusoe!

Musings With A Mirror

A coating of mercury behind a pane of glass
Just about the size of a human
Stood before me, as I stood before it!

It showed what it saw
And it saw the fullest me;
A bit of stubble and unkempt hair
Creases on the forehead,
Folded arms akimbo and legs apart
A challenging posture indeed.

Yet the mirror seemed to read more,
My sighs and deep breaths
Even my worries and queries:
A peek into my wounded and weary soul
The past scars and the pain with them

A full person emerging on it.
A quiet conversation started
The air between us seemed to vacate.

'You are broken within and without'
'I seem to be so, don't I?', I retort:'
I can see that, my friend, all of that'
'So that is me,' I draw up and conclude.

'You shall, as you choose to be.'
'What do you mean?' I ask, frowning more.
'Would you try something if I suggest?'
'I don't have to, yet I can try,' say I
'Take a breath and break a smile'
'This is simple, so I shall,' I reply.

I take a deep breath and put up a smile
The person in front of me does smile back.
'How does it feel and how does it look?'
'A bit lighter and a bit more handsome'
'Ha! Why don't you try something else, may be laugh?'
'I may look stupid, but I shall try.'

So, I laugh, this time aloud;
The person laughed but without a sound
'I heard you, but you can't me'
'Weird it is but wonderful more,' say I.
'That is, you, my dear friend, weird but wonderful.'
'And you were also the weary and worried.'

I walk away from the mirror and the conversation stopped
'Weary and worried' and yet 'weird and wonderful;'
The choice had been always mine.

Solace For The Soul

The soul seeks solace,
In the words of the song
From a different time and place
To make up for what does not belong
The unsaid words and deep sighs;
The distant stare and pursed lips

A silent facade and a stormy soul.
Are they storms in teacups?
For reasons not yet clear
The smiles have disappeared.
But things will be eventually fine
Just wait for the sun to shine!

The Universe Understands

Image by efes from Pixabay

If you make it your own, every element of the universe will understand and respond. Try it out.

> Even the evening walk in the gardens
> Welcomed with thunder drum rolls
> Celebrated by the celestial fireworks.
>
> As you rest on the park bench
> Washed by the ten-minute rain
> Pristine and clean for you!
>
> The clear twilight sky
> Makes a reservation for you
> In its billion-star hotel.
> The evening breeze blows

Switching on the air conditioner
Just mild to suit your moods.

And the white Daffodils nearby
Send a whiff of their scent
Just to add to the ambience.

The white blob in the sky
Has its dents and flaws;
Yet is an unceasing witness.

That the universe does understand
That you are the missing piece
Just created to witness its miracle.

PART 4
Little Dose for the Heart

Wild Thoughts

In the garden of the wild kind
I found a budding rose
Covered in the morning dew.

In my cluttered mind
A beautiful thought arose
And it was about you.

Between Music And Lyrics

Image by Gina Marie Vollendorf from Pixabay

Trapped between the notes;

Trapped between the words;

Moments of my existence

Snippets of silence

Vacuum between thoughts

Filled with my breath

And the sounds of my heartbeat

Somewhere and sometimes I do exist

In your memories.

That's good enough!

As the music and lyrics

Engulf and drown me

In your larger universe!

I Fell In Love

I fell in love
Only to rise again
Holding your hand
with you in my heart.

Dreaming of you
when I am awake
Being there with you
in your dreams.

Floating with you
Amid the stars
Sipping hot chocolate
On the cool white moon.

Lying on the beach
Looking at the blue skies

Watching the azure ocean
On an endless vacation.
Walking on the clouds
Touching the mist
Savoring the snow
At the tip of our tongues.

Traveling to the horizon
To watch the sun rise and set
Flying high in the sky
Living our lives without regret.

As we grow old together
Carrying those memories
In our hearts forever
I fell in love!

Just A Cuddle-And-Sleep

Holding your hands
Lying next to each other,
With your head touching mine
The warmth of your breath on my
face
And mine on yours
Your titillating hairs against my
face
That makes me sneeze
Or your warm feet touching mine
Your hands on my chests
And mine on your hips
Our eyes interlocked
And ...

And we lay still
It is the long night in silence
A journey beyond the moments
No words spoken nor heard

Only the heart beats flutter.
It is not lust, my dear
We don't toil or sweat
Just a cuddle and sleep
A form of embrace and just
The touches of companionship
Trust, friendship and love
Somewhere, the sky and the stars
Will wink at us and agree
That it is beyond the rights and
wrongs.

We lay there still
As the soundless clocks tick by
To wake up the sun
Who prods us with its sharp rays
To announce every morning
That our destination has arrived.

Butterflies & Hearts

How is that
You are the butterfly
but it is my heart
that flutters.

Sleeping With Monsters

There are nights I sleep without dreams
And there are nights in dreams I sleep!
The white light and the halo from the table lamp
That you never switch off because you are afraid
Of those invisible monsters that haunt in your sleep
And speak to you and you only;
I can neither feel nor hear them

Yet I wish I could, because I share your terror.
Finally we hug each other and you sleep
While I lay wondering how it would be to sleep;
Your monsters take a break while I stay awake
When the sun shines through the curtains
The table lamp fades away yet your sleep does not.
I am still awake to clear the garbage and boil the kettle.

The monsters come back when you are awake
I still cannot see them in broad day light.
They talk and torment you
I can only talk to you and not them
Yet you hold my hands and keep calm
Just because we feel that we have each other
Till another night comes and swallows the day.

Totem Sign

It is the moment
When you reflect in my eyes;
Yet I see only your lips move
The mellifluous voice heard;
But the words lost ... and lost...
(Here I stutter)
In my eternal trance
My fingers touch my face
To show my totem sign
That you are for real
And I am living my dream.

Surrogate Solace
(Radha Missing Krishna)

Without you, I am like those days
That nobody ever remembers, but I do
As I fill them with your memories –
A surrogate solace.

PART 5
THREE MEN ON A BENCH:
The Weird And Wonderful World

Three Men On A Bench

(Pic: Axis House, Mumbai, Courtesy :Ashok Subramanian)

Three old men sat on a bench,
At the corner of a nowhere park
Like rivers meeting at the estuary,
Living the last moments of their life.

Wrinkles and scars of the many seasons
Evidence of stories that they share–
Between them they travelled different paths

But time brought them together,
To forget the present
And remember the past.

Stories to cherish and memories to remember,
Sorrows and regrets that remain,
A small world of their own
In the frontier of their death
Three old men sat on a bench,
At the corner of a nowhere park.

Random Scribbles Of A Summer Vagabond
Aka One Empty Bench

The summer vagabond, am I?

Homeless but happy

And Free from the shackles

Of the hamster cage

Watch my Soulful eyes,

And peaceful soul

Empty pockets but

Rich smiles

Broad mind and

Deep sleep

Stopped watch for

Timelesstruth.

No identity and

No address

No bank account and

No tax to pay

A life lived

day by day

Summer by summer

And one day
It's an empty bench.

The full moon;
Early summer breeze;
Dancing shadows of trees;
The empty park bench;
Loads of silence;
That is my company.
Yours?
As I peep in
The window of the homefolks
I see stress.
Running the rat race,
Parental entitlement,
Branded by grades,
Sheep in a herd.
Job security.
Next generation comes,
Repeats the same.
When will you give up?

Come with me.
Let us sit on the empty bench.
With Vanilla ice cream
Wet and drenched.
In the sudden summer rain
Let us walk in the streets
Sipping hot ginger tea
Looking for an empty bench.

Live under the open skies
Under billion stars
Under the bright streetlights
Amid waging tails
and gnarling teeth
Watched by suspecting eyes.
And kicked by leather boots
Till all I leave behind
Is one empty bench.

Where Did It Start

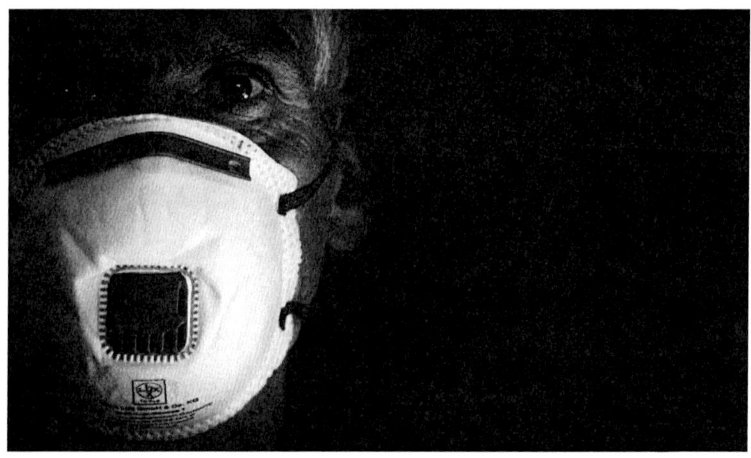

Where did it start
A touch or a sneeze
Or carried in the breeze.

A war is on
Deep within
Shown by scans
As lung lesions.

The body screams that
It needs its peace
Elevated temperatures
Which no words can cool.

Words of advice;
Words of caution;
The I-told-you-so's;

And where-did-you-get's.

Many helping hands
and a few wagging tongues;
The mind screams that
It needs its peace.
Ringing phones and loud words
Which only silence can sooth

Where will it end
A life past the disease
Or a life that would cease.

The scars of this war
Will remain etched:
If I live, in my memory,
If I die, in others.

Vultures And Crocs

Aren't we vultures

When we use the deceased

Without scruples

To feed our own

Materialistic desires?

A National Geographic

Movie in the making

Vultures turn victims

And shed croc tears.

Scars of yesterday

Shall remain tomorrow.

No suture can stitch

This ignominy.

Divide By Lines

Image by Thorsten Frenzel from Pixabay

Take a piece of land
And draw a line
And say it's mine.

Sing a song of the eons!
Make it the national anthem
And say it's us versus them.

Color a rectangle
Call it your national flag
Of which you boast and brag.

Raise men and give them guns
An army there, not a mere band

To defend the lines on the land.

Write a book of do's and don'ts
Name it the constitution:
A codebook of myriads
corrections.

Create a sense of ownership
Call the real estate a nation
And stoke patriotic passion.

Give a name and call it a nation
It is time to draw another line
And start all over again.

Her Noah's Arc

Shweta Hitesh Joshi inspired this poem. In a late night chat, she asked me, concerned, when some mothers were in the ICU, battling COVID. She asked me, 'Where is the Noah's Arc?' This poem is a tribute to a benevolent mind.

Image by Jeff Jacobs from Pixabay

'Noah's Arc,' remarked she.
'On board, are we?'
'Is this our turn?
Will we escape
The deadly churn?'

These Words of mine, Mark!
Noah built his Arc
With wood and ropes
But also indefatigable hope.

In the worsening storms
He remained calm
Didn't remember the strife

But yearned to save every life.
Little Noah's are inside us
Filled with benevolence
Stick to the indefatigable hope
That binds the wood and ropes.

Meadows, sunshine, and ponds
We shall again glimpse,
For, there is life beyond
This dreadful apocalypse.

Remains In The River

The souls that departed
Will never know
What happened to their remains!

But if they know
Would they weep in sorrow
Or laugh at the living
Who remain back on earth!
But have moved on
That they did not give
Dignity to the departed.

Would they feel ashamed
That they kicked the ladder
On their way to heaven?
The vehicle they travelled on earth
Floating and now bloated!

Would they feel satisfied
That they are feeding
The fishes in the river
Or the mongrels ashore?

Would they feel vindicated
That their pictures of their
remains
Flashed across the world
Throwing light on the horror?

Would they feel nothing at all
As they know now for sure
that is the way things were
Are and will be
And nothing can be changed?

Moments And Memories - The Karmic Cycle

Image by Schäferle from Pixabay

We walked on the beach

Hand in hand

Footprints on the beach sand

Erased by the waves.

The words we spoke

Music to our ears

Yet fade into thin air

Replaced by silence.

The moments that we create are

Erased and recreated as memories

A karmic cycle of every event

Performed by Time.

Life, You And Me

Image by Stocksnap from Pixabay

Life is a long sentence and death is the full stop–
Did I write these words for you to read and remember?
Would you, the one who loved me, miss me when I am not around?
For I would never know the aftermath on this earth.

I can feel today and now, remember the past,
And imagine the future - yet I won't know beyond this life.
When you read these words, I would be long gone,
To where I do not know, but you will remain.

When I close my eyes one final time never to open again
I can only think of these questions but cannot ask –
Will you regret those moments you were away from me?
Or cherish them till its your turn to leave?

The winks and the sighs, the smiles, and the weeps,
A bond that will break physically yet will remain
In memories as the movies of my life gone past
In my mind and yours, some savory, and others bitter

A white light welcomes me from the yonder;
My time has come, and I know I have to go
Yet I think about you, my lips curve into a smile
In those last moments, as I embrace the eternal cool bliss.

Events Of Today

I am a history buff.
Yet I don't understand wars. But History turns its page only when there is a war or strife, and it comes to us as events of today- like in Afghanistan.

Image by Amber Clay from Pixabay

History is incomprehensible
As events of today.
But the events of today
Would be history of the future.

Which is costlier we ask–
Peace or freedom?
Some say peace

As no one gets killed.
Some say freedom
As one would get to live.

So war is to fight,
To bring freedom or peace.
Yet it brings death and distress
To the innocent without a choice.

Stories of the past
Are quickly forgotten.
Each story is neither about
morality
Nor about good and evil.
It is never about the Gods
That they pray or hate
Even if in their names
They call out to fight.

It has been always about
agreements
Or irreconcilable differences.
It is about exertion of power
To achieve their own end.

May be it is just business as usual
For arms and ammunitions trade.
The strife of the people
Is the opportunity anew.

There are stories untold
Of the dying and the wounded
Precious childhood and dreams
lost
Forever in the melee.

Nobody counts the mortal
remains;
Yet history will find the mortar
remains
Of unexploded shells and
landmines,
Telling the story of an inglorious
past.

History is incomprehensible
As events of today.
But the events of today
Would be history of the future.

Death

Pic by le_petite_female at Pixabay.

Death is about cessation.
The blood stops flowing in the
veins.
The breath stops flowing through
our nostrils.

Death is about sleep.
It is a sleep for eternity.
Yet no dreams or nightmares.

Death is about senses.
No hunger or no thirst.
No feeling of warmth or cold.
Death is about time.
It is when we become the past.

And we can't think about the
future.

Death is about the silence.
The sound of the heart beat stops.
And no more words spoken or
heard.

Death is about letting go.
The heart lets go of its beat.
The body lets go of its life.
Death is about what remains.
The flesh and the bones.
The memories and the regrets.
Death is about the lies.

The goals that we chased.
The things we possessed.

Death is about the truth.
It is the full stop to our sentence.
It is the last page of the story we
write.

Death is freedom.
Freedom from the vicissitudes.
Freedom from the shenanigans.

Death is opportunity.
To pass on a legacy.
To create memories.

Death is success.
That you have passed your life.
That you are beyond the worldly
opinions.

Death is a failure.
Because no life is ever a failure.
And if it does not remind us to
live.

Death is about life.
It is about the others we leave.
It is about the life we lived.

On And Forward

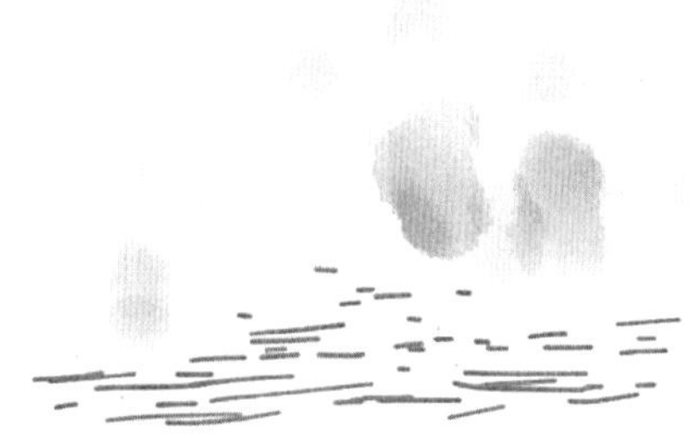

When a dear soul departs
Emptying eyes of tears
Leaving minds with memories.

It was a stop in our journey

Now the caravan has to move on
With that empty seat.
When the sun rises again,
We have to look forward
Because life goes on.

Don't Miss The Beat

Picture by Jarmaluk at Pixabay.

A world of poets, musicians and artists
Paintings and music, poems and prose;

Yet people walk past the beauties of creation
Diving into their phones and to catch the 8:30 a.m.
Bread and butter is what they are after.

Can they ever see that the notes and strokes
Cost nothing but time? Yet they won't

Unless they slow down, stare and listen,
Their souls are trapped in the drudgery of the routine.
Like the Schrodinger's cat, there is nothing to see or listen
For there is no art without an audience.

Another Boring Summer

The Neem is shedding fast;
The golden leaves blown away;
The hot air whooshes across;
Only the tired brown twigs
remain.

The pigeons court and copulate
Behind the humming air
conditioners;
While ravens crow, watching
them in disdain
While waiting for the leftovers.

Cows and dogs fight for their
space
Turning over the waste bin to
rummage;

While the day wager calmly
watches
As he sips special tea on credit.

The dry loose soil is thirsty
With the gardener long gone.
Perhaps he has no job
And rains are miracle in this city.

The grass once was green
Iis now glowing yellow.
But not charming but starving.
It is supposed to be green, stupid.

The watchman covers his face
with a wet cloth in the hope.
The breeze will make it cool.

There is no fan in his broken
cabin.

The cleaners rest in the empty car
parks
Rubbing their calloused hands.
Their brooms and shovels lay on
the side
Waiting for somebody to bring
lunch.

Somewhere up in the building
A kid orders an ice cream.
The couple order a kebab or a
pizza
Cursing the delivery charges and
delays.

Signals jumped amid cranking
horns

Yelling drivers at the poor
delivery person.
All that to avoid the yelling couple
When he knocks their door.

The woman upstairs turns on the
volume
As the actors blare in the
garrulous soap.
The next door slams hard to hide
the curses
As others wait for him to appear
on his video.

Another summer comes by this
city
To find that nothing has changed
Even the sun is tired to see
The same boring act all over
again.

In The Name Of War

Pic by pixel2013 in Pixabay

A war takes lives and livelihoods.

The fighters – young guys with guns – don't really know what they are fighting for, and why they are!

They see blood and gore, life ebbing away, limbs torn out of bodies!

The valor of the victors is only visible, for they get to tell the tale of their choice!

The vanquished disappear without a word, and sometimes, without even an epitaph!

The effect of the war carries on long after it's over.

Orphaned children, widowed wives and husbands, childless parents.

Limbless bodies. The unburied dead.

Years of hard work levelled by a shell from nowhere.

Human life takes refuge, shredding all its dignity.

Food and water, clean air and shelter, are now a distant dream.

They all know this—

A war they fight now will be erased by another war in the future.

The men at the top, are failed men, on both sides – for they led their kids to this futile feud.

The real war is with the vile of humanity.

History is a good teacher, only as long as there are students to learn.

They Are Waiting

Image by Leandro De Carvalho from Pixabay

How does a story shine
And characters come alive?
Either you read and imagine
Or watch them in a movie.

Whoever has seen the characters
Fell in love with them.
Yet it is an untold story
For many eyes and ears.

They are waiting
To sing and dance

To cry and copulate
To die and rise again.

In a different time
In a different land
They are waiting
To enact their tale.

In the unturned pages
Of the unread books
At the corner book store
And the neighborhood libraries.

Some Days And Other Days

Images by martinbinias of Pixabay.

Some days –

> Wet eyes and dry throats look at the blue sky
> The sun stares back in white anger and silence
> The beautiful skin of the soil is dry and cracked
> The tongues taste salty feeling the tears and sweat.

Other days -

> Layers of torn cotton soaked in grey dye
> No saline in their tears when they cry
> Even sadness tastes fresh in the heavens
> That the sun takes a quick swig behind the cloud curtains.
> Imagine what would pour if the Gods have so much fun
> And all that elixir drains unchecked into the oceans?

Some days again –

> Wet eyes and dry throats look at the blue sky
> The sun stares back in white anger and silence
> The beautiful skin of the soil is dry and cracked
> The tongues taste salty feeling the tears and sweat.